CHAPTER 1 – Double entry bookkeeping

1. Multiple choice questions [1 mark each]

i. Dale, a sole trader sold some used furniture for cash. Which entries in Dale's books will record this?

	Debit account	Credit account
A	Furniture	Cash
B	Cash	Sales
C	Furniture	Sales
D	Cash	Furniture

ii. Sam, a sole trader, purchases inventory from Tom on credit. Which entries in Tom's books will record this transaction?

	Debit account	Credit account
A	Purchases	Tom
B	Sales	Tom
C	Purchases	Bank
D	Sam	Sales

iii. Dewi, a sole trader, receives $600 rent from Wanda by a bank transfer. Which entries in Wanda's books will record the transaction?

	Debit account	Credit account
A	Bank	Wanda
B	Dewi	Bank
C	Rent	Bank
D	Bank	Rent

iv. The purpose of ledgers maintained by a business is **not**.
   A   to post transactions from the books of prime entry
   B   to help in the preparation of the income statement and statement of financial position
   C   to verify the accuracy of the double entry system of book-keeping
   D   to supply data for the preparation of the trial balance

2. Name the types of ledgers normally maintained by a business [3]

   ....

   ....

   ....

3. Define: [4]
   a. Sales

      ....

      ....

   b. Purchases returns

      ....

      ....

c. Nominal accounts

....

d. Cash discounts

....

....

4. Complete the following table by writing the word 'true' or 'false' against each statement [5]

Every business transaction results in two entries	
An account is where all the information about the business' objectives is collected	
The nominal ledger contains the personal accounts of a business's customers	
Furniture account is a real account	
Discounts allowed is a cash discount	

5. For each of the following transactions, decide which account will be debited and which account will be credited: [20]

20x9		Debit	Credit
Jun 1	The proprietor transferred $45,000 into the firm's bank.		
Jun 4	The proprietor borrowed $6,000 cash from Kalam.		
Jun 6	$1,000 was withdrawn from the bank for business use.		
Jun 9	Lenny, a customer paid $4,500 cash		
Jun 13	The business sold a used computer for cash $200		
Jun 18	The business bought a car for business use $13,000		
Jun 20	The proprietor paid his personal electricity bill $400 from the business bank account.		
Jun 24	The business bought stationery $250 paying by cheque.		
Jun 29	The business paid a supplier by bank transfer $700		
Jun 30	The business received a rent refund of $35 cash		

6. Enter the following transactions in the purchases ledger. [10]

Jan 1 Bought inventory from Hassan on credit $580.
Jan 5 Bought inventory from Janice for cash $340.
Jan 7 Bought inventory from Hassan on credit $600.
Jan 8 Returned inventory to Hassan $80.
Jan 25 Paid Hassan $1045 by cheque in full settlement of his account.

....

....

....

....

....

....
....
....
....
....
....

CHAPTER 2 – The Trial Balance

1. Multiple choice questions [1 mark each]
    i.   Which of the following accounts will normally have a debit balance?

    A   Trade receivables
    B   Capital
    C   Interest receivable
    D   Sales

    ii.   A company's trial balance shows debit balances in excess of credit balance by $1,000. What could explain this?
    A Cash overstated by $540; Omission of the telephone account totalling $460
    B Trade payables overstated by $450; Trade receivables understated by $550
    C Omission of accumulated depreciation of $500; sales understated by $500
    D Purchases understated by $500; omission of sales invoices totalling $500

    iii.   Which of the following errors affect the trial balance?
    A   An error of omission
    B   An error of commission
    C   A totalling error
    D   An error of original entry

    iv.   Which statement is correct?
     A Carriage inwards is a credit
     B Carriage outwards is a debit
     C Purchases returns is a debit.
     D Sales returns is a credit

2. Fill in the blanks   [5]

    A .... balance is a .... listing account .... and their

    balances in .... and .... columns as on a particular day.

3. Match items in column A with a corresponding item in column B [5]

A	B
A debit balance in a personal account	Credit balance
A credit balance in a personal account	Debtors
Sales account total is $45 more than it should be	Debit side more than the credit side in the trial balance
Drawings account was recorded but its corresponding entry, cash was not	creditors
A bank overdraft	Credit side more than the debit side in the trial balance

4. Complete the following table, writing 'true' or 'false' against each statement

Closing inventory appears as a credit in the trial balance	
The bank account can be a debit or a credit balance	
Opening inventory appears as a debit in the trial balance	
The cash account can be a debit or credit balance	
A trial balance will balance if double entries has been correctly made in the ledgers for each transaction.	

5. Give reasons for the following:

   i.   Closing inventory is not entered in the trial balance. [3]

   ....

   ....

   ....

   ....

   ....

   ii. A cash account is always a debit balance, but a bank account can be a debit or credit balance. [5]

   ....

   ....

   ....

   ....

   ....

   ....

   iii. The trial balance drawn up on April 1 will be different from a trial balance drawn up on April 5. [2]

   ....

   ....

   ....

   ....

iv.	A trial balance does not balance sometimes (3 reasons) [3]

	....

	....

	....

	....

	....

	....

CHAPTER 3 – Books of prime entry

1. Multiple choice questions [1 mark each]

i. Which of the following statements about a trade discount is correct?

A It is the discount given at the time of a purchase
B It is also known as Discounts received
C It is given for early payment
D It is shown in the three-column cash book

ii. Which of the following is **not** an example of a book of prime entry?

A The cash book
B The sales journal
C The sales ledger
D The journal

iii. A business has a bank balance of $4,800. It pays for materials invoiced at $3,000 less trade discount of 30% and a cash discount of 10%. A cheque for $450 is received from Mavis, a customer. What is the bank balance after these transactions?

A $ 2550
B $ 3360
C $3450
D $3,500

2. List five books of prime entry. [5]

....

....

....

....

....

3. Outline two uses of subsidiary books [2]

....

....

....

....

4. How is double entry completed when a credit entry takes place? [2]

....

5. Name 5 errors that do not affect the trial balance. [5]

....

....

....

....

....

6. Fill in the blanks with accounts that have to be debited and credited to **correct** the following errors: [10]

Errors	Account to be debited	Account to be credited
1. Repairs to a motor van are debited to motor van account.		
2. The sales account is overcast by $700 and the salary account is also overcast by $700.		
3. Samson paid us by cheque and we debited Samson and credited bank.		
4. We have debited bank and credited Massey's account with $650 instead of $560.		
5. Cash drawings of $900 had been credited to the bank column of the cash book.		

7. Circle the item/s would be posted from the books of prime entry to the ledgers if the business maintains a sales journal, a purchases journal and a cash book? [[2]
a. A provision for depreciation
b. The writing off of an irrecoverable debt
c. Interest charged on overdue accounts
d. Discounts allowed

8. **Draw up a three-column cash book from the following information:** [10]
20x5
June 1 Balances brought down from May : $
Cash   200
Bank   1,500
Trade receivable accounts:
Mason   400
Popcey   2,000
Abraham   800
Trade payable accounts:
Sulaiman   500
Ali   400
20x5
June 3 Mason pays us by cheque 380
June 5 We pay Ali cash 384
June 10 We withdraw cash from bank for business use 400
June 15 Abraham pays us his account in cash 787
June 22 We pay salaries by cheque 300
June 25 We pay Sulaiman cash 479
June 29 Popcey pays us by cheque 1,982

8

CHAPTER 4 – Income statements of sole traders

1. Multiple choice questions [1 mark each]

   i.   Which of the following should be treated as revenue expenditure in the accounts of a hotel?
   A Installation cost of a new alarm
   B Legal fees for debt collection
   C Legal fees incurred in the purchase of a hotel
   D Purchase of a computer

   ii.   You are given the following information for the year ended 31 December 20x9:

	1 Jan 20x9	31 December 20x9
Inventory	$6,000	$9,000
Trade payables	$8,000	$10,000

   Total payments to trade payables were $20,000.
   What is the cost of sales for the year ended 31 December 20x9?
   A $15,000
   B $19,000
   C $21,000
   D $25,000

   iii.   After draft accounts had been prepared, the following errors were discovered.
   Opening inventory was overvalued by $2,000
   Closing inventory was undervalued by $3,000
   If the original gross profit was $90,000, what was the gross profit after the errors were corrected?
   A $85,000
   B $89,000
   C $91,000
   D $95,000

2. Complete the following table by writing 'true' or 'false' against each sentence. [5]

	True/false
The trading account can be drawn up for a service business	
The Income statement lists the assets, liabilities and capital of a business	
The profit for the year is calculated in the income statement	
The gross profit is calculated in the trading account	
The expenses are listed in the trading account	

3. a. Pass the journal entries enable the balances of the Sales a/c $40,000, Sales Returns a/c $1,000, Opening Inventory a/c $4,000, Purchases a/c $20,000, Purchases Returns a/c $2,000 and Closing Inventory 6,000, to be transferred to the Trading account. Narratives not needed. [12]

   b. Draw up a trading account with the information above. [5]

   ....

   ....

   ....

   ....

....

....

....

....

....

4. Pass a journal entry to record the following:
   Larry took $780 worth of goods from the business for his own use. [2]

....

....

5. A company has the following figures for years 20x1 and 20x2:

	20x1	20x2
	$	$
Profit for the year	40,000	50,000
Cost of sales	120,000	180,000

It discovers that at the end of 20x1 the value of inventory was overstated by $8,000.
Calculate the correct Cost of Sales and profit for the year for:
   a. 20x1
   b. 20x2   [6]

....

....

....

....

....

6. Oscar gives you the following information for the year ended 31 December 20x6:

	Dr.	Cr.
	$	$
Opening Inventory	1090	
Purchases	4571	
Sales		7811
Carriage inwards	150	
Carriage outwards	70	
Purchases returns		500
Salaries	1000	
Rent and rates	170	
Discounts	48	17

Draw up an income statement for the year ended 31 December 20x6. [10]

....

CHAPTER 5 – Statement of financial position for sole traders

1. Multiple choice questions [1 mark each]

    i. Which of the following is correct?
        A Capital – Liabilities = Assets
        B Capital = Assets – Liabilities
        C Capital + Assets = Liabilities
        D Assets + Liabilities = Capital

    ii. Which of the following is correct?
        A Profit for the year = Opening capital + closing capital – drawings
        B Profit for the year = Closing capital – opening capital – drawings
        C Profit for the year = Opening capital + closing capital + drawings
        D Profit for the year = Opening capital – closing capital + drawings

    iii. Which of the following is correct?
        A Capital Employed = Opening capital - Profit for the year – Drawings
        B Capital Employed = Opening capital + Profit for the year + Drawings
        C Capital Employed = Non-current Assets + Current Assets – Current Liabilities
        D Capital Employed = Non-current Assets - Current Assets + Current Liabilities

2. Complete the following table by writing 'true' or 'false' against each sentence. [5]

	True/false
The statement of financial position reflects the accounting equation	
Working capital = Current assets – Current liabilities	
Current assets are listed in order of liquidity in the statement of financial position.	
The statement of financial position is used to calculate the profit for the year.	
The statement of financial will change from day to day	

3. How are balances in the Income Statement and Drawings Account transferred to the Capital Account at the end of the financial year? [6]

....

....

....

....

....

....

....

....

4. Draw up a statement of financial position from the following information for the year ended 31 December 20x7. [8]

	$
Lighting and heating expenses	3,000
Land and Property	130,000
Fixtures and fittings	5,000
Trade receivables	780
Trade payables	20,000
Cash at bank	45,000
Drawings	1,220
Capital	126,000
Profit for the year	40,500
Inventory at 31 December 20x7	4,500

....

....

....

....

....

....

....

....

....

....

....

....

....

....

....

CHAPTER 6 – Accounting principles

1. Multiple choice questions [1 mark each]

i. Which of the following items may be included in the statement of financial position at more than historical cost?
   A Research and development costs
   B Good will
   C Land and buildings
   D Work in progress

ii. The writing off of an irrecoverable debt is an example of the
   A substance over form principle.
   B prudence principle.
   C historic cost principle
   D going concern principle

iii. Which of the following is an example of the principle of substance over form?
   A not depreciating land and buildings
   B capitalising research costs
   C capitalising the cost of a machine bought on hire purchase
   D providing for expenditure not yet paid

iv. A company decides to change from the straight-line method to the reducing balance method when depreciating non-current assets. They are not following the principle of
   A Materiality
   B Going concern
   C Historic cost
   D Consistency

2. Define the following principles giving examples. [5]

i. Substance over form

   ....

   ....

   ....

   ....

ii. Going concern

   ....

   ....

   ....

   ....

15

iii.   Historic cost

....

....

....

....

iv.   Realisation

....

....

....

....

....

v.   Accruals

....

....

....

....

....

3.   What kind of information is not revealed by Accounting? [5]

....

....

....

....

....

....

....

....

....

4. A customer paid in advance $980 cash on 9 June 20x3 for goods that were to be supplied on 1 July 20x3. What are the entries to be made in the books of accounts? [2]

....

....

....

....

5. Answer briefly. [1 mark each]

i. When are sales recorded in the seller's accounts?

....

....

ii. Due to uncertainty about his business continuing, the proprietor is forced to make a large reduction in the valuation of his year-end stock. Which principle is being applied?

....

....

iii. Which concept is being applied if insurance paid in advance is shown in the statement of financial position as a current asset?

....

iv. A Business continues to depreciate its fixed assets at the same rate as the previous years in spite of falling profits. Which concept is being applied?

....

v. Which transactions are kept separate from those of a business?

....

vi. A provision for doubtful debts is being made in order to take into account foreseeable loses. Which principle is being applied?

....

....

vii. Accounts cannot use any other unit of measurement apart from money; which concept is being applied?

....

....

CHAPTER 7 – Accruals and prepayments

1. Multiple choice questions. [1 mark each]

i. Tom rents out office space to Jerry who owed $4,500 for rent at 31 December 20x8. However, he had paid $3,200 rent in advance in the year ended 31 December 20x9. During the year ended 31 December 20x9, Tom received $17,100 rent from Jerry. What is the rental income appearing in Tom's income statement for the year ended 20x9?
   A 15,800
   B 18,400
   C 24,800
   D 9.400

ii. Malika Ltd paid $15,000 for electricity in the year ended 30 June 20x2. At that date, accrued electricity expenses were $2,000. However, at 1 July 20x1 Malika Ltd had paid $1,000 in advance for electricity. Calculate the electricity charge for the year ended 30 June 20x2.
   A 15,000
   B 18,000
   C 17,000
   D 16,000

iii. Kent received rental income of $111,000 during the year ended 31 August 20x2. At 1 September 20x1 rent prepaid was $4,200 and $2,000 was owed to him by way of rent. At 31 August 20x2, $2,400 was accrued and $1,600 was prepaid. Calculate the total rent receivable for the year ended 31 August 20x2.
   A $114,000
   B $112,800
   C $111,000
   D $110,600

iv. An accrual of $375 was treated as a prepayment in the income statement of a sole trader's income statement. The profit for the year will be
   A Overstated by $375
   B Overstated by $750
   C Understated by $375
   D Understated by $750

v. Miron pays its rent in advance on the first day of each month. He has paid the following during the financial year ended 31 October 20x3:
   Up to and including 1 June $500 per month
   From 1 July $600 per month.
   Which of the following amount will appear in the financial statements for the year?

	Income statement	Statement of financial position
A	$7,000	
B	$6,400	
C	$6,400	$600 prepaid
D	$6,400	$600 accrued

2. Answer the following questions briefly. [2 marks each]

i. How is an accrued expense treated in the books of account?

....

....

....

....

....

ii. How is prepaid income treated in the books of account?

....

....

....

....

iii. What do the debit and credit balances in a consumables account signify?

....

....

....

....

3. Corina's financial year ends on 30 June 20-3. The trial balance on 30 June 20-3 included the following:

	Debit $
Rent	750
Insurance	50
Rates	140

At 30 June 20-3, Corina owed $45 for Insurance and $30 for Rates. $80 of the rent was prepaid.
Draw up:
a) Relevant extract of the Income Statement for the year ended 30 June 20-3
b) Relevant extract of the statement of financial position as at 30 June 20-3.   [4]

4. Dominic started trading on 1 May 2003. He paid rent on the following days:

Date	Period	Amount in $
2 May 20x3	1 May – 30 June	1,000
3 July 20x3	1 July – 30 September	1,500
2 October 20x3	1 October – 31 December	1,500
4 January 20x4	1 January – 31 March	1,560
1 April 20x4	1 April – 30 June	1,560

What is the amount that will appear as a prepayment in the year ended 30 April 20x4 for rent? [3]

19

....

....

....

....

....

....

....

5. Fill in the blanks: [6]

Opening balances:	Expenses	Income
Balance b/d (accrual)	Credit entry	....
Balance b/d (prepayment)	....	....
Closing balances:		
Balance c/d (accrual)	....	....
Balance c/d (prepayment)	....	Debit entry

6. A business paid $490 for stationery in the year ended 31 December 20x7. At that date, they owed $60 and had unused stationery of $30. Draw up a stationery account for the year ended 31 December 20x7. [4]

....

....

....

....

....

....

....

....

CHAPTER 8 – Depreciation of non-current assets

1. Multiple choice questions [1 mark each]

   i.   Which of the following is a reason to charge depreciation on non-current assets?
   A. To show when an asset has to be replaced
   B. To make sure that there is sufficient cash available to replace the asset
   C. To record the net realisable value of non-current assets in the statement of financial position
   D. To spread the cost of the assets over their estimated useful life.

   ii.   Lofty Ltd sold some furniture and made a profit of $70. The furniture cost $500 and accumulated depreciation from the sale at the date of the sale was $240. What was the furniture sold for?
   A. $190   B. $170   C. $330   D. $310

   iii.   Koolkat Ltd. bought IT equipment for $2,200 on 1 January 20x7. They aim to use it for 4 years and then sell it for $280. What is the depreciation charge for the year ended 31 December 20x8, using the straight – line method?
   A. $1,100   B. $960   C. $550   D. $480

   iv.   A machine was incorrectly depreciated for the whole year at 10% instead of 25% using the straight-line method. After the provision, the ledger balances were:
   Machinery at cost: $530,000
   Provision for depreciation: $53,000
   Which of the following entries will correct the error?
   A. Debit the provision for depreciation – machinery account with $132,500; credit the income statement with $132,500
   B. Debit the income statement with $79,500; credit provision for depreciation – machinery account with $79,500
   C. Debit the income statement with $132,500; credit provision for depreciation – machinery account with $132,500
   D. Debit provision for depreciation – machinery account with 79,500; credit income statement with $79,500

   v.   Alex depreciates his motor vehicles by 10% using the reducing balance method. What is the depreciation charge for the machinery bought for $40,000 in its second year of use?
   A. $3,600   B. $32,40   C. $3,200   D. $4,000

2. What is the profit or loss on disposal if an asset costing $120,000, with an accumulated depreciation of $72,400 is sold for $46,500 on credit. [3]

   ....

   ....

   ....

   ....

   ....

3. Give two reasons why provision for depreciation is made for a non-current asset. [5]

....

....

....

....

....

....

....

....

....

....

4. Give two reasons why non-current assets depreciate. [2]

....

....

....

....

....

....

....

....

5. Give two factors that would determine the choice of method between the Straight-Line Method and the Reducing Balance Method? [2]

....

....

....

....

....

....

....

6. A car was bought for $5500 on January 4th 20x0. Depreciation is calculated on the assets in existence at the end of the year using the straight- line method @10%. The asset was sold on 5th October 20x3 for $2000. Draw up the following accounts: [5]
a) Car a/c
b) Depreciation for Car a/c
c) The Disposal of Car Account

....

....

....

....

....

....

....

....

....

....

....

....

7. On June 1, 20x2, a Motor vehicle was purchased for $40,000. The cost was settled by a cheque payment of $34,000 and the part exchange of another motor vehicle for the balance. This motor vehicle had cost $25,000 and had accumulated depreciation of $13,000. at June 1, 20x2. Depreciation is charged in the year of purchase but not in the year of disposal.
Draw up the following accounts: [10]
a. Motor vehicle at cost
b. Provision for depreciation of motor vehicle
c. Motor vehicle disposal

....

....

....

....

....

....

....

CHAPTER 9 – Irrecoverable debts and Doubtful debts

1. Multiple choice questions. [1 mark each]

i. At 1 January 20x2 a company has a provision for doubtful debts of $1,000. At 31 December 20x2, the end of the financial year, the required provision is $2,500. During the Year debts of $1,500 are written off and $100 is received in respect of a debt written of many years ago. What is the net amount charged to the Income statement for irrecoverable and doubtful debts?

A $2,500   B $1,500   C $ 2,900   D $3,000

ii. The sales ledger balances at 31 December 20x3 are:

| Debit | $14,240 |
| Credit | $960 |

When preparing the annual accounts, it was decided to write off irrecoverable debts of $200 and to maintain a provision for doubtful debts at 2.5%. What will the provision for doubtful debts be at the year-end?

A $327   B $332   C $151   D $351

iii. A business increases its provision for doubtful debts by $1,600. What is the effect of this adjustment on the year-end statement of financial position?

	Profit for the year	Net trade receivables
A	Decreases by $1,600	Increases by $1,600
B	Decreases by $1,600	Decreases by $1,600
C	Increases by $1,600	Decreases by $1,600
D	Increases by $1,600	Increases by $1,600

2. Lew, a sole trader, gives you the following information:

His provision for doubtful debts account had a balance of $3,500 on 1 November 20x6. This was made up of a general provision of $2,000, which was 2% of all his trade receivables, and a further expected loss of $1,500, the total amount owed by Le Ching, who had been declared bankrupt.

On 30 November 20x6, Lew received $0.30 in the $ from Le Ching in full settlement of his debt. The remainder of the debt was written off.

On 30 April 20x7, Hui Jin, whose debt of $1,200 had been written off completely in 20x1, paid her debt in full in cash.

On 31 October 20x7 Lew adjusted his provision for doubtful debts account to 3% of all trade receivables: his total trade receivables outstanding at that date amounted to $110,000. There were no expected irrecoverable debts.

i. Draw up the following accounts in Lew's ledgers for the year ended 31 October 20x7: [8]
a. Provision for doubtful debts
b. Irrecoverable debts
c. Irrecoverable debts recovered

....

....

....

....

....

....

....

....

....

....

....

....

....

ii. State the effect on Lew's profit for the year of the change in the provision for doubtful debts. [1]

....

....

....

3a. Briefly explain three ways in which a provision for doubtful debts can be calculated. [6]

....

....

....

....

....

....

....

....

....

....

....

b. You are given the following information about Ramesh, Kenny and Moniz, all customers who owe the business money:

	1 July 20x7 $	30 June 20x8 $
Ramesh	750	-
Kenny	1,000	2,000
Moniz	-	1,500
	1,750	3,500
General provision	4,150	7,200
Total provision	5,900	10,700

During the year ended 30 June 20x8, Ramesh was declared bankrupt and a final payment of $50 was received. What is the charge to the profit for the year to 30 June 20x8 for provision for doubtful debts?   [2]

....

....

....

4. Answer briefly:

a. Give two reasons why a provision for doubtful debts is made. [2]

....

....

b. What is the difference between a provision and a liability? [2]

....

....

5. Fill in the missing figures in the following table:

Provision for doubtful debts for year 1	Provision for doubtful debts in year 2	Amount in Income statement in year 1	Amount in Income statement in year 2	Amount entered in the statement of financial position Year 1	Amount entered in the statement of financial position Year 2
$ 4,500	$5,000	....	....	....	....
$3,600	$2,600	....	....	....	....

6. A trial balance at 31 December 20x9, before making end of year adjustments, showed:

	$
Trade receivables	50,000 (Dr)
Provision for doubtful debts	700 (Cr)

At 31 December 20x9, it was decided to write off a debt of $5,000 and to make a provision for doubtful debts of 2% of trade receivables.
Calculate the total irrecoverable and doubtful debts expense for the year ended 31 December 20x9. [5]

....

....

....

....

....

....

7. Ziye Lee increases her General Provision for Doubtful Debts from 4% to 5% in the year ended December 31, 20x5. The following information is available:

	Year ended 31 December 20x7	Year ended 31 December 20x8
Trade receivables (These Included irrecoverable debts)	50,000	45,000
Irrecoverable debts	3,000	2,000
Doubtful debts	2,000	1,400

What is the effect on the general provision for doubtful debts in the year ended 31 December 20x8? [3]

....

....

....

....

....

CHAPTER 10 – Bank Reconciliation Statement

1. Multiple choice questions   [1 mark each]

   i.   Sam's bank account shows that his bank account is overdrawn by $10,136 on 31 December 20x7. At that date, cheques drawn on his account, but not yet presented to the bank, totalled $4,998 and cheques paid to his account, but not yet credited by the bank, totalled $5,896. His bank statement shows that interest of $181 has been charged, but this has not yet been entered in the cash book. What is the correct bank balance to be shown in the statement of financial position at 31 December 20x7?
   A $9,057 overdrawn
   B $9,238 overdrawn
   C $10,853 overdrawn
   D $11,034 overdrawn

2. Answer the following questions briefly. [2 marks each]
   i.   Give two reasons why the balance as per a bank statement of a business differs from the balance in the cash book of that business.
   ii. What is a bank overdraft?
   iii. What are the uses of a Bank reconciliation statement?

3. Draw up a bank reconciliation statement from the following details as at 31st December 20x3: [4]

	$
Cash at bank as per bank column of the cash book	800
Unpresented cheques	280
Cheques paid into the bank but not yet entered in the bank statement	350
Credit transfers entered on the bank statement but not in the cash book	100
Cash at bank as per bank statement	830

....

....

....

....

....

....

....

....

4. The Cash Book of Mala showed a balance of $200 at the bank as on December 31, 20x5. On the same date the bank statement balance was $80 (Debit). On comparing the Bank Statement with the Cash Book the following information was revealed:
i) A cheque for $450 lodged with the bank had not been cleared for payment.
ii) A cheque for $200 sent to a creditor had not been presented for payment.
iii) Bank charges of $30 were omitted from the cash book.
Required:
a) Calculate the correct Cash Book Balance at December 31, 20x5. [3]

....

....

....

....

....

....

b) Prepare a bank reconciliation statement at December 31, 20x5. [5]

....

....

....

....

....

....

....

....

CHAPTER 11 – Control Accounts

1. Multiple choice questions. [1 mark each]
   i. Arden's sales journal has been overstated. Which adjustment will be required as a result of this error?

	Sales ledger control account	List of sales ledger balances
A	Cr	No change
B	Cr	Reduce
C	Dr	Reduce
D	Dr	No change

   ii. A purchases ledger control account has a closing balance of $92,460. A debtor for $720 transferred from the sales ledger has been entered on the wrong side of the purchases ledger control account. What is the correct balance on the purchases ledger control account?

   A $93,900

   B $91,020

   C $91,740

   D $93,180

   iii. You are given the following information:

	$
Sales returns	1,150
Credit sales	16,810
Discounts allowed	276
Increase in trade receivables	5,406
Increase in provision for doubtful debts	600
irrecoverable debts written off	100

   How much cash was received from trade receivables during the month?

   A $9,878   B $10,154   C $20,690   D $9,278

   iv. Llama ltd. gives you the following information regarding its Purchases Ledger Control account for the year ended 31 August 20x4:

	$
Balances at 1 September 20x3: Credit	20,000
Debit	4,000
Transactions during the year:	
Total of suppliers' invoices	45,000
Discounts received	500
Credit notes received	1,500
Sales ledger contra	5,000
Balances at 31 August 20x4: Credit	23,000
Debit	Nil

   How much cash did the company pay its suppliers during the year?

   A $31,000   B $34,000   C $35,000   D $54,000

   v. The following is an extract from the trial balance of Kwame, a sole trader at 30 April 20x6.

	Debit	Credit
	$	$
Sales ledger control account	38,600	800
Purchases ledger control account	1,300	26,800

A purchases invoice for inventory received on 29 April 20x6 for $1,000 was omitted from the purchases ledger control account.

Which figure should appear in the statement of financial position?

A $25,500   B $27,600   C $27,800   D $28,600

vi. Zane buys from and sells goods to Jafari. Zane owes $3,200 to Jafari and Jafari owes $1,941 to Zane. An agreement is in force for the sales ledger account and purchases ledger account balances to be offset, so that only one payment is made. Which double entry records the offset in Zane's books?

		Dr	Cr
		$	$
A	Purchases ledger control account	3,200	
	Sales ledger control account		3,200
B	Jafari's (purchases ledger) account	1,941	
	Sales ledger control account		1,941
C	Purchases ledger control account	1,259	
	Sales ledger control account		1,259
D	Purchases ledger control account	1,941	
	Sales ledger control account		1,941

2. State **two** advantages of preparing control accounts. [2]

....

....

....

....

3. State why a sales ledger control account may have **both** a debit **and** a credit closing balance. [1]

....

....

....

....

4. a. Prepare Jaicheng Li's sales ledger control account for the month of October from the following information: [8]

	$
Total sales ledger balances at 1 October 2018	18,423
Total purchases ledger balances at 1 October 2018	16,667
Cheques received from customers	141,876
Cheques paid to suppliers	92,118

Credit sales	185,265
Credit purchases	107,223
Irrecoverable debts	2,054
Discounts allowed	5,812
Discounts received	3,444
Sales returns	2,535
Purchases returns	1,990
Customer's cheque dishonoured	350
Debit balances transferred from the sales ledger to the purchases ledger	1,046

....

....

....

....

....

....

....

....

....

....

b. The balance on the sales ledger control account at 31 December is $61,752. This does not agree with the total of the list of sales ledger balances on that date, which amounts to $61,500.

On checking the accounts, the following errors are discovered:

1. A balance of $198 has been omitted from the list of sales ledger balances at 31 December.
2. A customer's account has been undercast by $325.
3. A sales invoice for $2,520 has been completely omitted from the books.
4. The sales figure for the month should have been listed as $230,256, **not** $230,265.
5. A customer who owed the business $280 has been declared bankrupt. This has been correctly entered in the control account, but no entry has been made to cancel the debt in the customer's personal account.

i. Make the necessary entries in the sales ledger control account to correct it. [3]

....

....

....

....

....

....

ii. Prepare a statement amending the total of the sales ledger balances. [4]

....

....

....

....

....

....

....

CHAPTER 12 – Suspense accounts and Incomplete records

1. Multiple choice questions [1 mark each]
   i. The balance on the Sales Ledger Control account amounting to $54,000 has been entered in the trial balance as $45,000. The difference on the trial balance has been entered in a suspense account. Which journal entry is required to correct the error?

	Account to be debited		Account to be credited	
A	Suspense account	$9,000	-	
B	Suspense account	$9,000	Sales Ledger Control account	$9,000
C	Sales ledger Control account	$9000	Suspense account	$9,000
D	-		Suspense account	$9,000

   ii. The person who kept the books of Kwame, a sole trader, has disappeared. There is no cash in the till and theft is suspected. The following information is available:

	$
Cash in hand at 1 January 20x4	750
Total cash sales from 1 January to 31 December 20x4	150,000
Decrease in trade receivables during the year ended 31 December 20x4	5,500
Receipts from customers paid into the bank	96,000
Expenses paid from cash received	5,000

   How much has the bookkeeper stolen during the year ended 31 December 20x4?
   A $55250   B $60,250   C $44,250   D $49,750

   iii. After draft accounts were prepared, the following errors were discovered.
   Opening inventory was overvalued by $2,000
   Closing inventory was undervalued by $3,000
   If the original gross profit was $90,000, what was the gross profit after the errors were corrected?
   A $89,000   B $91,000   C $95,000   D $85,000

   iv. You are given the following information for the year ended 31 December 20x7
   Balances at 1 January 20x7:   Inventory $6,000; Trade payables $8,000
   Balances at 31 December 20x7:   Inventory $9,000; Trade payables $10,000
   Payments to suppliers during the year were $20,000.
   What is the cost of sales for the year ended 31 December 20x7?
   A $ 25,000 B $15,000   C $19,000   D $21,000

2. Elise's annual inventory-taking normally takes place on May 31, the last day of her financial year. However, for the year ended 31 May 20x1, the inventory-taking was only completed on 7 June 20x1 by an inexperienced member of her staff. Elise felt that the inventory figure of $92,050 was too low and on investigation, discovered that the following had occurred during the week ended 7 June 20x1 which had not been accounted for in the closing inventory calculation.
   a. Goods with a selling price of $1,040 had been sent to a customer on approval.
   b. Goods costing $9,400 were received and invoiced.
   c. Sales of $18,760 had been made and invoiced to customers.
   These sales included:
   i. An overcharge of $160
   ii. Sales of $6,000 on special offer at a margin of 10%
   iii. Damaged goods which had cost $2,500 and were sold for $2,800.
   Elise's standard rate of gross profit is 25% of sales.
   Calculate the correct value of closing inventory at 31 May 20x1. [15]

....

....

....

....

....

....

....

....

....

....

3. Leslie plans to go into business on 1 July 20x4 and has a start-up capital of $60,000 that he will deposit into a business bank account. He plans on using this money to purchase premises costing $44,000 and office furniture costing $5,000. His business plan reveals the following information:

Projected sales for the year ended 30 June 20x5 are $140,000 of which 80% will be cash sales. Sales commission will amount to 4% and discounts allowed will be 1.5% of total sales. Irrecoverable debts will be 2.5% of credit sales.

He plans to achieve a gross margin of 40% and a profit margin of 20%.

He will depreciate his furniture using the Reducing Balance method at 45%.

His suppliers will give him a discount of 2.5% of all purchases. All purchases are credit purchases.

Wages will be $13,250 and Sundry expenses $6,600. There will be no accruals or prepayments at 30 June 20x5.

He plans on drawing $5,000 plus 5% of total sales.

At 30 June 20x5, his projected balances will be: $

                              Inventory   16,000

                              Trade receivables 6,000

                              Trade payables   5,000

The closing balance at bank is not estimated.

Calculate:

i.   Purchases [2]

....

....

....

....

....

....

ii.   Payments to suppliers [3]

....

....

....

....

....

iii.   Receipts from customers [4]

....

....

....

....

iv.   Draw up a projected Income Statement for the year ended 30 June 20x5. [7]

....

....

....

....

....

....

....

....

....

....

....

....

v. Draw up a projected Statement of Financial Position for the year ended 30 June 20x5. [5]

....

....

....

....

....

....

....

....

....

....

....

....

....

....

4. Fill in the blank spaces: [1 mark each]
a. Profit for the year = ... capital – .... capital + ... – Capital introduced
b. Credit sales for the year = ... balance of trade receivables + cash received from ....+.............. debts + discounts .... - ....balance of trade receivables.
c. Total sales = ... + ...
d. Credit purchases = cash paid to .... + discounts .... + ... balance of trade payables - .... balance of trade payables.
e. If the mark-up is 25% then the margin is ....

5. List 2 advantages of maintaining full financial records   [2]

....

....

....

....

CHAPTER 13 – Valuation of inventory

1. Multiple choice questions [1 mark each]
i. Saraf Ltd. sells goods on sale or return at a mark-up of 25%. The following information is available at 31 December 20x1.

	$
Inventory at the warehouse at cost	300,000
Inventory sent on sale or return at invoice price	200,000

What will appear in the statement of financial position at 31 December 20x1 as closing inventory?

A $ 500,000   B $300,000   C $460,000   D $450,000

ii. Inventory – taking of a company was completed on 6 August 20x8 instead of at the end of the financial year on 31 July 20x8. Inventory was valued at 6 August 20x8 at $86,500. The following information is available:

	$
Sales (at cost)	1,750
Purchases	1,550
Returns Inwards at cost	310
Returns outwards	190

What is the value of inventory on the company's statement of financial position at 31 July 20x8?

A $86,580   B $86,820   C $86,420   D $86,180

iii. A damaged product originally cost $15 per unit but can only be sold at the selling price of $22 after modifications costing $14 per unit. At what valuation is the product shown in the statement of financial position?

A $15 per unit   B $14 per unit   C $8 per unit   D $22 per unit

2. Answer the following questions briefly.
a. Give the formula for calculating Net Realisable Value [1]

....

....

b. Omar sells five different grades of products. The following are the costs and net realisable value of these grades. Fill in the blank spaces: [7]

	Cost	NRV	Value to be used for inventory valuation
	$	$	$
Grade 1	900	970	....
Grade 2	1,100	1,080	....
Grade 3	600	640	....
Grade 4	370	400	....
Grade 5	1,900	2,000	....
	4,870	5,090	....

c. Name two methods used to value homogeneous inventory. [2]

....

....

39

d. State one advantage and one disadvantage of using FIFO [2]

....

....

....

....

e. State one advantage and one disadvantage of using AVCO [2]

....

....

....

....

3. At 30 April 20x4, inventory of a certain product consisted of 300 units which had cost $2.10/unit. The receipts and sales of the product in May were as follows:

Date		Receipts (Units)	Price per Unit ($)	Issues (Units)
May 1	b/f	300	2.10	
5		30	2.00	
10				100
15		200	1.90	
19				120
23		150	2.00	
29				110

Calculate the value of inventory at 31 May 20x4 using
a) FIFO
   i. Using the perpetual method [5]

....

....

....

....

....

....

....

....

ii. Using the periodic method [4]

....

....

....

....

....

    b)   AVCO [5]

....

....

....

....

....

....

....

....

CHAPTER 14 – Partnerships

1. Multiple choice questions [1 mark each]
i. M and N are partners sharing profits equally. They admitted P as a partner and profits were to be shared equally. Goodwill was valued at $18,000. What is the effect of this change on the capital account balance of M?

A Decrease of $6,000   B Increase of $3,000   C Decrease of $3,000   D Increase of $6,000

ii. Interest charged on partners' drawings should be
   A Debited to the income statement
   B Credited to the income statement
   C Credited to the appropriation account
   D Debited to the appropriation account

iii. You are given the following information about a partnership.

	$
Drawings	10,000
Interest on partner's loan to firm	1,000
Profit for the year before interest	15,000
Interest on capital accounts	2,000

Which profit figure is to be appropriated between the partners?
A $15,000   B $14,000   C $3,000   D $13,000

2. Adira, Bibi and Dalia were in partnership sharing profits and losses equally. They do not operate current accounts. On 30 June 20x2 their capital account balances were:
   Adira $40,000
   Bibi $30,000
   Dalia $15,000

a. Bibi retired from the partnership on 1 July 20x2 and at that time goodwill was valued at $24,000. Non-current assets were revalued as follows:
   Property and equipment increased in value by $10,000
   Furniture and fittings increased in value by $4,000
   Motor vehicles decreased in value by $2,000
   They decided not to show a Goodwill or Revaluation account in the partnership books.
   Bibi received cash for her share of the partnership and Adira and Dalia continued to run the partnership still sharing the profits equally. Drawings during the year ended 30 June 20x3 were: Adira $46,000; Dalia $45,000
   The profit for the year was $120,000. Draw up the partners' capital accounts for the year ended 30 June 20x3 in columnar form. [11]

....

....

....

....

....

b. Rafa joined the partnership on 1 December 20x3, bringing in capital of $12,000 and $8,000 as her share of goodwill. No goodwill account was opened. Profits were now shared on the following basis: Adira 3/7; Dalia 3/7; Rafa 1/7
During the year ended 30 June 20x4, the profit for the year was $140,000 and the partners' drawings were: Adira $52,000; Dalia $48,000; Rafa $20,000. Profits accumulate at a regular rate throughout the year. The partnership was sold on 1 July 20x4 for $126,000. The partnership was dissolved, and all of the partners took the money due to them. Draw up the partners' capital accounts for the period 1 July 20x3 to 1 July 20x4 in columnar form. [14]

....

....

....

....

....

....

....

....

....

....

....

....

....

....

3. Complete the following table by writing the word 'true' or 'false' against each statement.

	True/False
Goodwill is unrealised profit.	
Unrealised profit is entered in the partners' current accounts.	
Goodwill is a tangible non-current asset.	
Interest on a partner's loan appears in the appropriation account.	
A Partner's salary appears in the appropriation account.	

4. Answer the following questions:
a. Give two advantages and two disadvantages of a partnership type of business as compared to that of a sole trader. [4]

....

....

....

....

....

....

....

....

b. List three items that would appear in a partner's current account. [3]

....

....

....

....

c. List three items that appear in a partnership deed. [3]

....

....

....

....

....

....

....

CHAPTER 15 – Accounts of Limited Companies

1. Multiple-choice questions [1mark each]

i. Rana ltd. is a company that has issued non-cumulative preference shares and ordinary shares. Which of the following statements is true?
A Preference shareholders may get a dividend.
B If no preference dividend is paid, it is carried forward to a future year.
C Preference shareholders always get a dividend.
d Preference shareholders and ordinary shareholders always get a dividend.

ii. Yu Yan Ltd. with an existing issued capital of 400,000 $1 ordinary shares, made a 1-for-5 bonus issue. This was later followed by a 1-for-3 rights issue which was fully subscribed.
What will be the balance on the share capital account after these transactions?
A 640,000   B $613,333   C $400,000   D $480,000

iii. Fardin Ltd. gives you the following information for the years ended 31 December

	20x4	20x5.
	$m	$m
Ordinary shares of $1 each	100	130
Share premium account	60	80

Further information:
a.   On 1 July 20x5 there was a bonus issue of 1 for every 10 shares
b.   On 1 October 20x5, there was a rights issue.
c.   There are no other reserve balances.
How much cash was received from the issue of shares in the year ended 31 December 20x5?
A $60m   B $30m C $20m   D $50m

iv. A shareholder in Saba Ltd. sells his shares to another person. What is the effect on the Share Capital Account of Saba Ltd.?
A It remains unaltered.
B It is increased by the market price of the shares.
C It is reduced by the face value of the shares sold.
D It is increased by the premium paid for the shares.

v. Wang Shu Ltd. has issued 8% debentures. What is the effect on the company's profit for the year and current assets in the year of the issue?

	Profit for the year	Net current assets
A	Decreases	Decreases
B	Decreases	Increases
C	Increases	Decreases
D	Increases	Increases

vi. Which of the following should be subtracted from the profit for the year to arrive at the cash balance?
A Increase in inventories
B Issue of new share capital
C Depreciation for the year
D Decrease in trade receivables

2. Feng Mian Hills PLC is a company which has been financed by the issue of the following shares and debentures:

2,000,000 Ordinary shares of $1 each $2,000,000
1,000,000 8% Preference shares of $1 each $1,000,000
500,000 5% Debentures of $1 each $500,000

a. During the year ended 31 August 20x7, the total distributable profits before payment of debenture interest was $300,000. The full $300,000 was paid out in debenture interest and share dividends. Calculate the percentage dividend paid to ordinary shareholders. Ignore taxation. [4]

....

....

....

....

....

....

....

b. Another company Nian Zhen PLC, which is similar to Feng Mian Hills, is financed as follows:

1,000,000 Ordinary shares of $1 each $1,000,000
2,000,000 8% Preference shares of $1 each $2,000,000
500,000 5% Debentures of $1 each $500,000

If Nian Zhen made the same profit for the year ended 31 August 20x7, what percentage would be paid to its ordinary shareholders? [3]

....

....

....

....

....

....

c. i) State and explain whether it is better to be an ordinary shareholder or a preference shareholder during times of falling profits? Assume that all available profits are distributed. [2]

....

....

....

ii) State **two** differences between:
Ordinary shares and debentures. [2]

....

....

....

....

3. Oaktree PLC's trial balance for the year ended 31 October 20x1 is given below.

	Dr $000	Cr $000
Bank	46	
Provision for depreciation on non-current assets		100
Trade receivables and payables	200	83
400,000 Ordinary shares of $1 each		400
200,000 10% Non-redeemable Preference shares of $1 each	200	
5% Debentures (20x5 – 20x7)		120
Loan from Neem Tree Finance		25
Retained earnings		20
Sales		970
Inventory at 1 November 20x0	80	
Non-current assets at cost	900	
Purchases	240	
Wages	230	
Irrecoverable debts written off	8	
Rent	65	
Provision for doubtful debts		2
General expenses	36	
Advertising	68	
Debenture interest	3	
Dividend on preference shares	20	
Interim dividend paid on Ordinary shares	24	
	1,920	1,920

Additional information:
i.   Interest on the loan was payable at 8% per annum.
ii.   Closing inventory was valued at $50,000.
iii. Depreciation is to be provided on all non-current assets at 20% using the reducing balance method.
iv.   Prepaid advertising amounted to $4,000.
v.   Wages due but unpaid totalled $8,000
vi.   Provision for doubtful debts to be increased to $6,000.
vii. $10,000 to be transferred to general reserve.
viii. A final dividend of $24,000 to be paid on ordinary shares.

a. Draw up the Income statement for Oaktree PLC for the year ended 31 October 20x1.[10]

b. Draw up a Statement of changes in equity for the year ended 31 October 20x1. [5]

....

....

....

....

....

....

....

c. Draw up a statement of financial position as at 31 October 20x1. [8]

....

....

....

....

....

....

....

....

....

....

....

....

....

....

....

4. A company's statement of financial position includes the following extract:

Share capital and reserves:	$
100,000 ordinary shares of $0.50	50,000
50,000 5% preference shares of $1	50,000
Share premium account	20,000
General reserve	10,000
Retained profit	2,000

Calculate the statement of financial position value of one ordinary share. [3]

....

....

....

5. Give **one** difference between:
a. A public limited company and a private limited company [2]

....

....

....

....

b. A limited company and other forms of business organisations [2]

....

....

....

....

....

c. Liabilities, provisions and reserves [3]

....

....

....

....

....

....

....

d. Capital reserves and revenue reserves [2]

....

....

....

....

e. Ordinary shares and preference shares [2]

....

....

....

f. The income statement and statement of cash flow. [2]

....

....

....

....

....

CHAPTER 16 Analysis and interpretation

1. Multiple choice questions [1 mark each]

i.   Syafiq PLC has a current ratio of 2:1 and a quick ratio of 0.5:1. What is the effect on
        the two ratios, if the company uses cash to purchase inventory?

	Current ratio	Quick ratio
A	decrease	decrease
B	no change	decrease
C	no change	increase
D	decrease	increase

ii.   The draft accounts of Nurul Ltd. included the following:
        Turnover $280,000
        Gross profit $60,000
        It was subsequently discovered that closing inventory was understated by $10,000.
        What will be the gross profit margin after this error is corrected?
        A 21.4%   B 17.9%   C 25%   D 20.7%

iii.   Mary Fernandes, a sole trader gives you the following information:
        Opening inventory $10,000
        Cost of sales $ 200,000
        Rate of inventory turnover 10 times.
        What is the value of the closing inventory?
        A $30,000   B $10,000   C $40,000   D $20,000

iv.   The trial balance of a company included the following figures:

	$
Credit sales	250,000
Cash sales	125,000
Returns: cash sales	6,000
Returns: credit sales	8,000
Trade receivables	38,000
Other receivables	12,000

        What is the Average Collection period?
        A 51 days   B 55 days   C 38 days   D 57 days

v.   How is a company best able to reduce its working capital in the short term?
        A   by reducing the time taken to pay its suppliers.
        B   by disposing of some surplus non-current assets.
        C   by decreasing the rate of inventory turnover.
        D   by reducing the trade receivables turnover period by offering discounts.

2. Huiwen gives you the following financial information for the year ended 31 May 20x2:
    Mark-up = 33.33%
    Rate of inventory turnover = 10 times
    Trade receivable turnover = 91.25 days
    Operating expenses to revenue ratio = 13.75%
    Current ratio = 1.67:1
    Acid test ratio = 1.33:1
    Non-current asset turnover = 3.33 times
    Additional information:
    Inventory at 31 May 20x2was $12,500

Cash sales which was 20% of total revenue was 40,000.
Trade receivables and trade payables balances were unchanged since 1 June 20x1.
Cash and cash equivalents was $10,000
Finance costs (interest owing) was $12,500
Calculate:
a. Gross profit [3]

....

....

....

....

....

b. Cost of sales [2]

....

....

....

....

....

c. Inventory at 1 June 20x1 [3]

....

....

....

....

....

d. Operating expenses [2]

....

....

....

....

....

e. Purchases [3]

....

....

....

....

....

f. Trade receivables [3]

....

....

....

....

....

g. Trade payables (rounded up to the nearest $1,000) [3]

....

....

....

....

....

h. Non-current assets at book value (rounded up to the nearest $1,000) [3]

....

....

....

....

....

3. Answer briefly.
a. Explain two uses of ratios [2]

....

....

....

....

....

....

b. Name two stakeholders of a business [2]

....

....

c. Explain two precautions that should be taken when comparing the ratios of two businesses. [4]

....

....

....

....

....

d. Explain two limitations of accounting statements. [4]

....

....

....

....

e. Give an example of: A profitability ratio   [1]

....

CHAPTER 17 – Absorption, Unit, Job and Batch costing

1. Multiple choice questions. [1 mark each]

i. Which of the following may result in an over-absorption of overheads?
A Expenditure in excess of budget
B Absorption based on actual expenditure and actual activity
C Expenditure below budget
D Activity below budget

ii. Emily confectionaries Ltd. gives you the following information:

	Department X	Department Y
Allocated heating expenses	$6,000	$14,000
Area in square metres	30,000	20,000

Rent for the year $100,000.
Which amount for rent and heating should be attributed to X?
A $72,000   B $62,000   C $56,000   D $66,000

iii. Tasya Women's hospital budgets for overheads totalling $11.5 million for a financial year. It expects to treat 25,000 patients in a year and each patient stays an average of 10 days. The hospital absorbs overheads on a patient/day basis. The annual direct costs are budgeted at $25 million. What is the overhead absorption rate?
A $460 per patient day
B $46 per patient day
C $100 per patient day
D $146 per patient day

2. Azeez is a sole trader who manufactures television sets which he sells for $250 each. He produces 60,000 units per annum, all of which are sold. At this level of production, the unit costs are:

	$
Direct materials	150
Direct labour	10
Variable overheads	10
Fixed overheads	15

Calculate the annual profit or loss [4]

....

....

....

....

....

....

....

3. Sodiq PLC uses AVCO as their system of inventory costing. Information about the raw material used during the month of November 20x5 are given below.

Date	Activity	Kg	Price per Kg	Job Number
1 Nov	Balance	3,000	$12.00	
3	Purchases	4,000	$12.10	
4	Issued	5,000		Job 23
8	Purchases	6,000	$12.20	
14	Issued	1,000		Job 24
16	Issued	3,000		Job 23
18	Purchases	5,000	$12.30	
23	Issued	3,000		Job 25
25	Issued	1,000		Job 23
26	Purchases	10,000	$12.20	
27	Issued	5,000		Job 25
28	Issued	3,000		Job 24

a. Calculate the total material cost on each job, rounding off to the nearest $100. All jobs were begun and completed in the November 20x5. [10]

....

....

....

....

....

....

....

....

....

....

....

....

....

....

....

....

b. Budgeted fixed costs for the year amounted to $4 per direct labour hour.
Other data relating to **Job 24** was as follows:
Job 24 was completed by one employee in 200 hours. 160 of these were at the basic rate of $8,80 per hour and the remainder was overtime paid at time-and-a-half (1.5 times the basic rate). Variable overheads totalled $650.
Calculate the profit on Job 24 if the profit to sales ratio is 25%. [8]

....

....

....

....

....

....

....

....

....

....

....

....

....

....

4. Abeba Limited manufactures three products for the motor vehicle industry, AL10, AL 20 and AL30. The company has four departments: assembly, machining, stores and canteen. The following information is available for one unit of the three products.

	AL10	AL20	AL30
Direct materials	$10.10	$12.50	$15.20
Direct labour hours – machining ($5.40 per hour)	50 mins	30 mins	40 mins
Direct labour ours- assembly ($7.50 per hour)	15 mins	10 mins	12 mins
Machine hours – machining	30 mins	20 mins	30 mins
Machine hours – assembly	10 mins	10 mins	15 mins

Estimated overhead costs for the year ended 31 December 20x6 are:

	$
Indirect wages	350,000
Machinery maintenance	80,000
Machinery insurance	8,000
Rent and rates	66,000
Buildings insurance	10,800
Machinery depreciation	25,500

Additional information:

	Machining	Assembly	Stores	Canteen
Number of indirect employees	8	16	4	2
Floor area in square metres	8000	9000	2000	1000
Value of machinery ($000)	300	150		
Number of orders from stores	5000	1500		
Budgeted labour hours	6800	35000		
Budgeted machine hours	45000	2500		
Use of canteen	30%	55%	15%	

a. Apportion the costs to the four departments and re-apportion the service departments' costs to production departments using a suitable basis. [10]

	Basis $	Machining $	Assembly $	Stores $	Canteen $
Indirect wages					
Machinery maintenance					
Machinery insurance					
Rent and rates					
Buildings insurance					
Machinery depreciation					
Reapportionment of canteen					
Reapportionment of stores					

b. Calculate appropriate absorption rates for each production department correct to two decimal places. [4]

....

....

....

....

....

....

....

The actual results for the year were:

	Machining	Assembly
Factory overheads	$300,000	$250,000
Direct labour hours	8,500	30,000
Direct machine hours	50,000	2000

c. Calculate the under or over absorption of overheads for each production department. [4]

....

....

....

....

....

d. Explain the reason for the over or under absorption of overheads calculated for **each** production department in part **(c)**. [2]

....

....

....

....

Additional information

e. Abeba Limited has been asked to prepare a quotation for a customer who requires 300 units of AL20. The company requires a gross profit of 40% on **each** order. Calculate the quoted selling price. [6]

....

....

....

....

....

....

....

....

....

....

5. Explain the following terms with respect to overheads.

i. Allocation [2]

....

....

....

....

ii. Apportionment [2]

....

....

....

....

iii. Absorption [2]

....

....

....

....

CHAPTER 18 – Marginal costing

1. Multiple choice questions [1 mark each]

i. A product whose fixed costs are $80,000 is sold for $100 per unit. Variable costs are 60% of the selling price. What is the break-even sales revenue?
A $2,000   B $1334   C $200,000 $13,334

ii. How can the total contribution from a given activity be calculated?
A Total sales – total profit
B Total sales + total fixed costs
C Total fixed costs + total profit
D Total direct costs – total profit

iii. Vivaan Ltd makes 500 units of a product and sells them at $50 each. The direct labour costs $2,500 and direct material costs $7,500. The fixed overheads are $8,400. If Vivaan Ltd increases its production to 600 units, how much profit will it make?
A $11,600   B $9,600   C $11,600   D $10,100

iv. Assuming that all other factors remain unchanged, the break-even point of a business can be lowered by increasing its
A fixed costs
B marginal costs
C budgeted sales
D selling prices

v. What is shown by this graph?

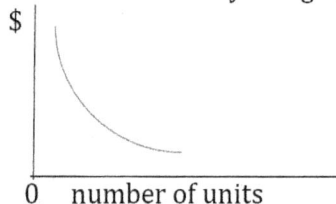

A fixed costs per unit
B variable costs per unit
C semi – variable costs per unit
D selling price per unit

vi. Divya Ltd. manufactures and sells a product X. In order to increase profitability, the ' directors are considering buying in the product X instead of manufacturing them.
 Divya Ltd. should buy product X from an outside supplier if the price is
A more than the total cost but less than the selling price.
B more than the marginal cost of production but less than the marginal cost of sales
C less than the marginal cost of production.
D more than the marginal cost of sales but less than the total cost.

vii. Selwyn, a sole trader manufactures a single product and sells it for $20 per unit. The variable costs are $15 per unit and the budgeted fixed costs per annum are $200,000. How many units must the company sell to make a profit for the year of $50,000?
A 50,000 units   B $10,000 units   C 30,000 units   D 40,000 units

viii. Julie confectionery PLC has sales revenue of $192,000, fixed costs of $40,000 and a contribution to sales ratio of 1/3. They make a profit of
A $88,000   B $24,000   C $50,667   D. $64,000

2. Ericson PLC produces products A, B and C. They give you the following information:

Product	A	B	C
Contribution per unit	$160	$175	$190
Fixed overheads per unit	$125	$130	$160
Labour hours per unit	1	1.25	0.75
Raw materials per unit	5kg	3kg	2kg

The company is experiencing a shortage of labour. In which order should the production of products be ranked to maximise profits? [2]

....

....

....

....

....

....

3. Jefferson Plc is a small company manufacturing Product T18. They give you the following information.

Sales in units	6000	12,000
	$	$
Direct materials	18,000	36,000
Direct labour	6,000	12,000
Production overheads	33,000	45,000
Administrative overheads	27,000	27,000

The company sells each product at $12 each. Calculate the break-even point in units. [4]

....

....

....

....

....

4. State **two** assumptions which are made when using break-even charts. State **one** limitation of each assumption. [4]

....

....

....

....

....

....

....

....

....

....

5. Aimee wraps PLC gives you the following information:
Output 600 units, all of which are sold at a price of $7.50 each. Variable costs are $2.50 per unit and the fixed cost is $1,000.

    a. Calculate the break-even point in **both** units and values. [5]

....

....

....

....

....

....

    b. State the Margin of Safety in both units and values. [2]

....

....

....

....

    c. Calculate the profit if the business sold 800 units but the fixed costs were increased by 20%. [4]

....

....

....

....

6. Nomalanga PLC manufactures Product X76. They use marginal costing and give you the following budgeted information for two years.

	Year 1	Year 2
	$	$
Direct labour	34,000	32,900
Direct materials	22,400	26,800
Factory costs	12,200	14,200
	Units	Units
Sales	10,000	11,000
Production	12,000	13,000

Additional information:

a. Of the factory costs $5,000 are fixed for each year and the remainder are variable.

b. Variable selling costs are expected to be 2% of the sales revenue for each year.

c. There was no opening inventory in year 1.

d. The selling price per unit is $20.

e. Variable cost per unit is not expected to change.

f. Fixed selling costs are $3,500 for year 1. These are expected to increase by 4% for year 2.

i. Calculate the budgeted variable cost of production per unit. [2]

....

....

....

....

....

ii. Calculate the **total** budgeted contribution for **each** year. [6]

....

....

....

....

....

....

....

iii. Calculate the budgeted production cost **per unit** for **each** year. [2]

....

....

....

....

....

....

....

....

....

Nomalanga PLC is considering using absorption costing.
iv. Calculate the **total** budgeted profit for **each** of the two years using absorption costing. [7]

....

....

....

....

....

....

....

....

....

v. Explain why profit calculated using absorption costing would be different to profit calculated using marginal costing. [3]

....

....

....

....

....

CHAPTER 19 – The Application of Accounting to Business Planning

1. List **five** benefits of accounting to businesses. [5]

....

....

....

....

....

....

2. Explain **two** advantages of budgets to a business. [4]

....

....

....

....

....

....

....

....

3. What are **two** disadvantages of budgeting? [4]

....

....

....

....

....

....

....

....

www.ingramcontent.com/pod-product-compliance
Lightning Source LLC
Chambersburg PA
CBHW061106210326
41597CB00022B/3994